CW00871742

BEDTIME PRAYERS FOR PROTECTION

PRAYING GOD'S WORD FOR A PEACEFUL SLEEP

BY **FEBORNIA ABIFADE**

ILLUSTRATED BY **i CENIZAL**

Tellwell Talent
www.tellwell.ca

ISBN
978-0-2288-7835-3 (Hardcover)
978-0-2288-7833-9 (Paperback)
978-0-2288-7834-6 (eBook)

In the beginning was the **Word**
(Jesus Christ), and the **Word**

(Jesus Christ) was with God, and the **Word**
(Jesus Christ) was God.

Now, the **Word** *(Jesus Christ)* is very near you; it
is in **your mouth** *(when spoken, it activates the
power of God)* and in **your heart** *(transformation
occurs)* so you may obey it.

For I command you today to love the LORD your
God, to walk in obedience to him, and to keep his
commands, decrees and laws; then you will live and
increase, and the LORD your God will bless you in
the land you are entering to possess.

John 1:1, Deuteronomy 30:14, 16 (NIV)

As you speak the Word *(Jesus Christ)* of God, *(from the Bible)* with your mouth *(out loud so, that, it activates),* you are drawing Jesus Christ nearer to you and your child. Therefore, speak it daily, consistently, in all circumstances, situations, and locations.

Please note that the italicized text in parentheses is intended to expand on the Word of God for understanding purposes. In the second section of this book, the blank parentheses in the prayers are intended for your child's name.

TABLE OF CONTENTS

LETTER TO PARENTS

Dear Parent,

This book is divided into two parts. The first part is for you, so that you can understand how to use the book effectively. The second part consists of targeted prayers for the child. Once you grasp the principles from section one, then you can resort to the subsequent bedtime prayers in section two.

The book is intended for parents who wish to protect their child at night, and for parents who wish to build a visual understanding of the Word of God in the mind of the young child. However, the core purpose of this book is to resolve the problem of children who suffer from nightmares. As a mother, I know how heart-wrenching it feels when you are awoken by the cries of your child who has had a bad dream. If it is a regular occurrence, you can be left feeling completely deflated and powerless.

The Word of God gives us the assurance and confidence that if we seek I AM WISDOM, every challenge can be placed under our feet. We stand victorious.

This book presents God's Word as a weapon of war to fight on your child's behalf and to give you victory over the wiles of the enemy.

May the Lord Jesus Christ protect you and family in Jesus name.

As a mother or father there is power in your faith and love in God. This faith and love will offer protection for your child. For this purpose, I encourage you with these examples from the Old Testament and the New Testament.

From **Exodus 2:2 (KJV)**,

And the woman conceived and bare a son: and when she saw him that he was a goodly child, she hid him three months.

From **Matthew 15: 21-28**,

21 Then Jesus went thence, and departed into the coasts of Tyre and Sidon.

22 And, behold, a woman of Canaan came out of the same coasts, and cried unto him, saying, Have mercy on me, O Lord, thou son of David; my daughter is grievously vexed with a devil.

23 But he answered her not a word. And his disciples came and besought him, saying, Send her away; for she crieth after us.

24 But he answered and said, I am not sent but unto the lost sheep of the house of Israel.

25 Then came she and worshipped him, saying, Lord, help me.

26 But he answered and said, It is not meet to take the children's bread, and to cast it to dogs.

^{27} And she said, Truth, Lord: yet the dogs eat of the crumbs which fall from their masters' table.

^{28} Then Jesus answered and said unto her, O woman, great is thy faith: be it unto thee even as thou wilt. And her daughter was made whole from that very hour.

Through these two examples above, we can see the love and desire of the mother to protect and seek deliverance for her child. In the case of Moses' mother, Jochebed, her desire was to hide her child. Can you imagine how challenging it must have been to hide a newborn child for three months?

And what about a father, you may ask? The Lord shows us that the desire and love for a child from either parent can bring deliverance. In this scripture, the father elicits the assistance of Jesus' disciples for help, and when they could not help, he strove to seek the master himself – Jesus Christ.

From **Mark 9: 14-29,**

[14] And when he came to his disciples, he saw a great multitude about them, and the scribes questioning with them.

[15] And straightway all the people, when they beheld him, were greatly amazed, and running to him saluted him.

[16] And he asked the scribes, What question ye with them?

[17] And one of the multitude answered and said, Master, I have brought unto thee my son, which hath a dumb spirit;

[18] And wheresoever he taketh him, he teareth him: and he foameth, and gnasheth with his teeth, and pineth away: and I spake to thy disciples that they should cast him out; and they could not.

[19] He answereth him, and saith, O faithless generation, how long shall I be with you? how long shall I suffer you? bring him unto me.

²⁰ And they brought him unto him: and when he saw him, straightway the spirit tare him; and he fell on the ground, and wallowed foaming.

²¹ And he asked his father, How long is it ago since this came unto him? And he said, of a child.

²² And often it hath cast him into the fire, and into the waters, to destroy him: but if thou canst do any thing, have compassion on us, and help us.

²³ Jesus said unto him, If thou canst believe, all things are possible to him that believeth.

²⁴ And straightway the father of the child cried out, and said with tears, Lord, I believe; help thou mine unbelief.

²⁵ When Jesus saw that the people came running together, he rebuked the foul spirit, saying unto him, Thou dumb and deaf spirit, I charge thee, come out of him, and enter no more into him.

²⁶ And the spirit cried, and rent him sore, and came out of him: and he was as one dead; insomuch that many said, He is dead.

²⁷ But Jesus took him by the hand, and lifted him up; and he arose.

²⁸ And when he was come into the house, his disciples asked him privately, Why could not we cast him out?

²⁹ And he said unto them, This kind can come forth by nothing, but by prayer and fasting.

However, before we begin our prayers, we must understand that I AM Jehovah Nissi has principles and precepts that must be followed in order for the King of Glory, the Mighty Man in Battle, to fight on our behalf.

Firstly, we must confess all known and unknown sins before the Lord as explained in 1st John 1:9.

If we confess our sins, He is faithful and just to forgive us our sins and to cleanse us from all unrighteousness.

Secondly, we must come into his presence with thanksgiving and praise as directed by Psalm 100:3-4. In so doing, God is inclined to listen to our prayers and to answer.

Psalm 100: 3-4

Know ye that the Lord he is God: it is he that hath made us, and not we ourselves; we are his people, and the sheep of his pasture.

Enter into his gates with thanksgiving, and into his courts with praise: be thankful unto him, and bless his name.

How To Prepare Your Child For A Peaceful Sleep

As the parent, you will be praying targeted prayers to hide your child in God's promises of his hand, rock which is Jesus Christ, pavilion, wings, the secret place of his presence, fire, his blood, and Christ Jesus.

Prepare the toddlers with reminders of bath and reading time. You could gently say "Clean up time, followed by bath time in ten minutes."

It is critical for youth to form a routine which is followed by the parent. Due to our evolving times, it has become harder to monitor what our children are exposed to daily within our home. For example, we are now teaching our children via online learning and in some instances the child could operate several applications on their laptop screen simultaneously. Technology is such that our children can divide their monitor into several applications: one web application on school work, one on virtual forums with friends, and another on games. It is important to note that not all games are suitable for developing minds. Some of these games can quite easily be the cause of your child's nightmares. As a parent, we need to monitor what our children are watching even more stringently because most content can have an adverse effect on their dream life.

How do you effectively implement these principles?

Start by removing all distractions of the world from the child at least one hour before bedtime. For example, turn off the television, and ask your child to put away all their electronic games and gadgets. This may be challenging at first, but you can start with fifteen minutes and gradually build it up to an hour. Within the hour, give the child their bath and have praise music playing in the background. As the parent, you must lead by example; you must show your child how to enter into the presence of God. Give thanks to God, sing praises, and confess your sins. Complete this entire process in the presence of your child. Remember, children learn through what we *do* more than what we say. *We* are their first carbon copy to mimic.

The key principle to teaching a child is repetition and consistency. Therefore, take one song and ensure you sing it every night. Encourage your child to sing along. If your child is not able to talk yet, still encourage them because with time they will sing along. Also teach them the name of Jesus and ask them to repeat his name. In the spiritual realm, Jesus' name is a powerful weapon to be victorious.

Beloved, I wish for you to read this book in the child's sleeping surroundings. I need you to be animated, and to show them what each word means in relation to their environment.

For example, if you have young toddlers, walk around their bed to demonstrate the fire of God around them, or roar as the Lion of the Tribe of Judah. In so doing, as they read along with you, the imprint of God's Word will resonate in their inner man. If any power of darkness appears in their dream, their inner man is now equipped to know what to say and do in the spiritual realm.

Ask youth questions to engage their interest such as: "Can you describe what a wall of fire could look like around your bed?" "Can you show me how Jesus can hide you in the palm of his hand?"

Teach them to agree with the prayers by allowing them to say "Amen." Teach them to say "Jesus." The Word of God says:

Psalm 8: 2 (NIV)

Through the praise of children and infants you have established a stronghold against your enemies, to silence the foe and the avenger.

Thanksgiving, praise, and prayers of a child are extremely potent to destroy the works of God's enemies for your child's angels are in God's presence continuously.

Matthew 18:10 (NIV)

10 "See that you do not despise one of these little ones. For I tell you that their angels in heaven always see the face of my Father in heaven.

Psalm 127: 4-5 KJV

4 As arrows are in the hand of a mighty man; so are children of the youth.

5 Happy is the man that hath his quiver full of them: they shall not be ashamed, but they shall speak with the enemies in the gate.

1st John 4:4 ESV

4 Little children, you are from God and have overcome them, for he who is in you is greater than he who is in the world.

Please confess God's Word out loud.

Psalm 103: 1-5 KJV

Bless the LORD, O my soul: and all
that is within me, bless his holy name.

² Bless the LORD, O my soul, and forget not all his
benefits:

³ Who forgiveth all thine iniquities; who healeth all
thy diseases;

⁴ Who redeemeth thy life from destruction; who
crowneth thee with lovingkindness and tender
mercies;

⁵ Who satisfieth thy mouth with good things; so that
thy youth is renewed like the eagles.

"I AM THE BREATH OF LIFE, I thank you. I thank
you for your mercy and grace upon my life and upon
('s) life. I thank you for your loving kindness
and tender mercies towards us. I thank you for your
help, protection, provision, love, and support. Lord,
I exalt your name. Take all the glory in our lives in
Jesus' name."

PRAISE SONG

Thank you, Lord, for saving my soul.

Thank you, Lord,
for saving my soul.

Thank you, Lord,
for making me whole.

Thank you, Lord,
for giving to me.

Thy great salvation
so rich and free.

(repeat twice)

SCRIPTURE CONFESSION

Each night before beginning the prayers, place your right hand on your child's pillow and read the following scriptures out loud. This will charge the child's room with the Word of God. Do this every night until you notice a change in the child's sleeping pattern.

Isaiah 49: 24-26 KJV

²⁴ Shall the prey be taken from the mighty, or the lawful captive delivered?

²⁵ But thus saith the LORD, Even the captives of the mighty shall be taken away, and the prey of the terrible shall be delivered: for I will contend with him that contendeth with thee, and I will save thy children.

²⁶ And I will feed them that oppress thee with their own flesh; and they shall be drunken with their own blood, as with sweet wine: and all flesh shall know that I the LORD am thy Saviour and thy Redeemer, the mighty One of Jacob.

Blessed is he that considereth the poor: the LORD will deliver him in time of trouble.

² The LORD will preserve him, and keep him alive; and he shall be blessed upon the earth: and thou wilt not deliver him unto the will of his enemies.

³ The LORD will strengthen him upon the bed of languishing: thou wilt make all his bed in his sickness.

⁴ I said, LORD, be merciful unto me: heal my soul; for I have sinned against thee.

⁵ Mine enemies speak evil of me, When shall he die, and his name perish?

⁶ And if he come to see me, he speaketh vanity: his heart gathereth iniquity to itself; when he goeth abroad, he telleth it.

⁷ All that hate me whisper together against me: against me do they devise my hurt.

⁸ An evil disease, say they, cleaveth fast unto him: and now that he lieth he shall rise up no more.

⁹ Yea, mine own familiar friend, in whom I trusted, which did eat of my bread, hath lifted up his heel against me.

¹⁰ But thou, O LORD, be merciful unto me, and raise me up, that I may requite them.

¹¹ By this I know that thou favourest me, because mine enemy doth not triumph over me.

¹² And as for me, thou upholdest me in mine integrity, and settest me before thy face for ever.

¹³ Blessed be the LORD God of Israel from everlasting, and to everlasting. Amen, and Amen.

Why You Must Call On The Name Of Jesus

Quite simply, there is no power that is greater than the POWER in the name of Jesus. Tonight, we will be praying to the Creator who created everything. He is mighty and strong. He will protect your child through the night, as his power is above everything both visible and invisible. The Bible advised us in his Word:

Psalm: 62:11 (NIV)

[11] One thing God has spoken, two things I have heard: "Power belongs to you, God."

Philippians 2:9-11 (NIV)

Therefore God exalted him to the highest place and gave him the name that is above every name,

[10] that at the name of Jesus every knee should bow, in heaven and on earth and under the earth,

[11] and every tongue acknowledge that Jesus Christ is Lord, to the glory of God the Father.

Colossians 1:15-17 (NIV)

[15] The Son is the image of the invisible God, the firstborn over all creation. [16] For in him all things were created: things in heaven and on earth, visible and invisible, whether thrones or powers or rulers or authorities; all things have been created through him and for him. [17] He is before all things, and in him all things hold together.

Colossians 2: 9-10

[9] For in Christ all the fullness of the Deity lives in bodily form,

[10] and in Christ you have been brought to fullness. He is the head over every power and authority.

The final task for the 'sacrificial praying parent' is morning devotion. This is where you will set aside time in the morning, solely to praise God. The best time for morning devotion is between the hours of 4 a.m. – 6 a.m. before anyone else gets up.

At first, this may be extremely challenging, if your child is up throughout the night after an attack. You have spent the entire night up with the child consoling and encouraging the child to go back to bed. As the parent, you may only get between two and three hours of sleep yourself.

Therefore, this final stage must be phased in gradually. It should be your ultimate goal. To clarify, the first stage of your sacrificial prayer is to stop the attack. The second phase is your morning devotion to deliver your child.

Your early morning praise devotional to God will deliver the child permanently.

Your early morning praise devotional consists of:

1. Thanking God for his goodness, kindness, love, protection, provision, and deliverance. Thank him for the breath of

life and protection for yourself and household. Name each item one by one from the smallest to the greatest.

2. Confess your sins and that of your forefathers. Often our bloodline is tainted with sin and we need to seek God's forgiveness.

3. When praising God, it is important to know that your praise is more powerful when using the old hymns or singing the hymns from the Book of Psalms. I strongly recommend using Volumes- 5, 6 and 9 of Esther Mui's Psalms. You can access these songs on YouTube or purchase them via her website. Your devotional should be a minimum of thirty minutes, but ideally sixty minutes. Extend it to the length that is comfortable for you. A key point is: "Don't ask God for anything," but if you strongly feel you need to, make a single request to God. We must trust that God is all-knowing, because often what we think we need is not what God knows we need.

4. Finally, thank him and take a short nap. One of these two scenarios may occur: Firstly, you may not go through the entire four steps above especially if you have been up all night. You may naturally fall asleep whilst praising. During your sleep time, God will reveal something to you. Therefore, always have a note-pad close by to quickly record the event of the dream you just had. Secondly, if you completed the entire process above, you can either continue with your day or take a short nap. The short nap will allow God to communicate to you through dreams. Do this consistently and he will show you the deliverance of your child. You will know when your child is delivered as your child will sleep peacefully throughout the night without the need of the prayers.

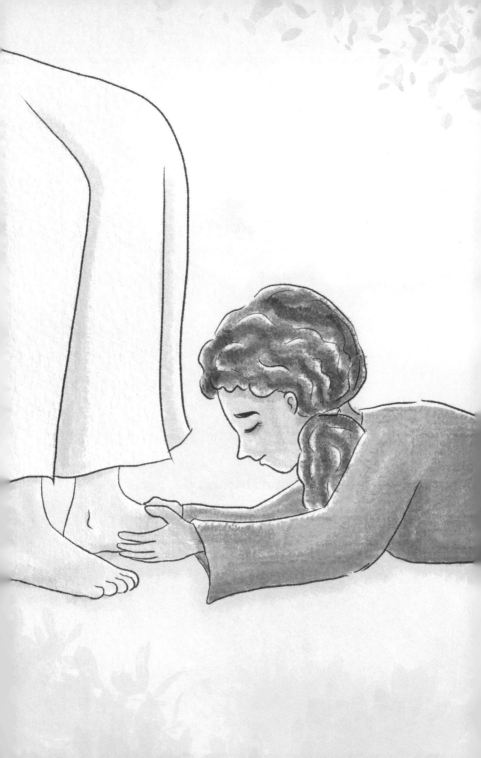

The heavens are thine, the earth also is thine:
as for the world and the fulness thereof,
thou hast founded them.

The earth is the LORD's, and the fulness thereof; the
world, and they that dwell therein.

I am the LORD, and there is none else, there is no
God beside me:

That they may know from the rising of the sun, and
from the west, that there is none beside me. I am the
LORD, and there is none else.

I form the light, and create darkness: I make peace,
and create evil: I the LORD do all these things.

Psalm 89:11; Psalm 24:1; Isaiah 45:5, 6-7

Lord God, you have created everything for your
will and purpose. Father, I thank you
for giving me

(   ), a beautiful gift from God. I dedicate him/
her to you this night and ask for your divine
protection as he/she goes to sleep
in the name of Jesus.

And it shall come to pass, while my glory passeth by, that I will put thee in a cleft of the rock, and will cover thee with my hand while I pass by.

The eternal God is thy refuge, and underneath are the everlasting arms: and he shall thrust out the enemy from before thee; and shall say, Destroy them.

Exodus 33:22; Deuteronomy 33:27,

O God my Father, put ( ) in a cleft of the rock of Jesus Christ and cover ( ) with your hand in Jesus' name. For your name, Lord is a refuge and strong tower for ( ) in Jesus' name.

In the shadow of his hand hath he hid me, and made me a polished shaft; in his quiver hath he hid me.

I have covered thee in the shadow of mine hand, that I may plant the heavens, and lay the foundations of the earth, and say unto Zion, Thou art my people.

Isaiah 49:2, 51:16

Lord Jesus, hide (   ) in the shadow of your
hand in the name of Jesus.

For I, saith the LORD, will be unto her a wall of fire round about, and will be the glory in the midst of her.

For our God is a consuming fire.

Zechariah 2:5; Hebrews 12:29,

Lord, be a wall of consuming fire round about
(   ) as he/she goes to bed this night. Watch over
him/her day and night in Jesus' name.

Keep me as the apple of the eye; hide me under the shadow of thy wings.

From the wicked that oppresses me, from my deadly enemies, who compass me about.

He shall cover thee with his feathers, and under his wings shalt thou trust; his truth shall be thy shield and buckler.

Psalms 17:8-9, 27:5, 32:7, 32:20, 62:2, 91:4, 119:114

My Father, keep (   ) as the apple of your eye; hide (   ) under the shadow of your wings. Cover (   ) with your feathers and hide (   ) under your wings in Jesus' name.

And one of the elders saith unto me, Weep not: behold, the Lion of the tribe of Judah, the Root of David, hath prevailed to open the book, and to loose the seven seals thereof.

And they sung a new song, saying, Thou art worthy to take the book, and to open the seals thereof: for thou was slain, and hast redeemed us to God by thy blood out of every kindred, and tongue, and people, and nation.

And hast made us unto our God kings and priests: and we shall reign on the earth.

Revelation 5:5, 9-10

Lion of the Tribe of Judah, roar at the works of darkness coming against (   ) this night, in the name of Jesus. The Lamb that was slain, for mankind, have mercy on (   ). Deliver (   ) by your blood in the name of Jesus.

For ye are dead, and your life is hid with Christ in God.

But the Lord is faithful, who shall establish you, and keep you from evil.

I will both lay me down in peace, and sleep: for thou, Lord, only makest me dwell in safety.

Colossians 3:3; 2nd Thessalonians 3:3, Psalm 4:8; Job 11:18-19,

Blood of Jesus, shield (   ), tonight in the name of Jesus. Blood of Jesus, hide (   ) in Christ Jesus, in the name of Jesus. Blood of Jesus, protect (   ) from all evil in the name of Jesus.

(   ), you will both lay down in peace and sleep, for thou Lord only makes you dwell in safety. Let the light from God's face shine down upon (   ) as he/she sleeps in Jesus' name.

If as a parent, you are not born again and don't know Jesus Christ, the effectiveness of these prayers will not be fully manifested. Therefore, you have an opportunity today to accept him as your Lord and Saviour. Confess this statement:

Lord Jesus, I accept your sacrifice on the cross. I thank you for dying for me. I acknowledge that I am a sinner. Help me, save me, and wash me in your blood. I confess you, as my Lord and Saviour. I declare that I am born again. I am a new man/ woman and my sins are forgiven. Fill me with the Holy Spirit and write my name in the Book of Life in the name of Jesus.

Finally, beloved, I pray that as you put these principles into practice that the Lord Jesus Christ will honour his Word in your child's life in Jesus' name.